GUNS

DON'T

OWN

US/A

by Rebecca Taylor

Introduction

As an extra introductory note, I wrote most of this piece prior to COVID-19. This book first began seven years ago, when I resolved to do my part to fight gun violence, when I was reeling from the news of twenty first-grade children being gunned down in school, along with their principal and several teachers. We see things through a very different lens these days, as a pandemic continues to rage through our country, and a powerful new civil rights movement has arisen. In fact, it has been this this current moment that has catalyzed me to bring this work forth. This work is significantly scaled back from other iterations I had envisioned. This work is much shorter and to the point. And though I am a published author, this piece is self-published. I decided seven years has been long enough. It is time to bring what I have now to the surface. And this may be just the beginning. The path my writings take will reveal itself in time.

For years we have heard gun control, gun control – over and over and over again. Just hearing this phrase can be all it takes to put us at each other's throats. When the whole time we're arguing about "gun control" – we've lost sight of what really has the control: the guns.

Yet there are those who say guns are just inanimate objects and that "guns don't kill people, people kill people." That makes about as much sense as saying money doesn't buy things, only people buy things. As if people could buy things without money or something else of value. By that logic, how can money, an inanimate object, buy anything? It's what it's deployed by people to do. Same with guns. We deploy them to kill. That's what they are made to do. Now whether we use a gun to kill a deer, a person or a crowd of people – that's what has heightened guns' control over society. Guns are not merely weapons now. They have been heightened to the level of false idols.

Rather than gun control, I believe more in stopping guns from controlling US/A. They are controlling both. Why do my son and so many children of his generation have to know what a code red drill even is, let alone do them? In my schools, the worst we ever had were fire drills.

We live in Condition Orange today, most of us. We live under the heavy weight of knowing a mass shooting could happen anywhere, anytime. We live in a strange hybrid of Wild West which might be even worse than living in the outlaw world of the past. At least they knew better what to expect then. Although it didn't solve gun violence, citizens were allowed to walk around armed. Now we live under a false sense of security. Cameras everywhere, going through the third degree just to get on a plane, most of our privacy stripped away often in the name of defending the country. Yet how did all of this extra security protect the scores of innocent citizens, many of them children, from the gun-wielding mass murderers who killed them?

The guns are out there now. Most of their owners will not give them up. But must we resign ourselves to the vicious cycle of mass shootings, the false appearances of action/change, "thoughts and prayers," only for society to snap back to the status quo, acting like the shooting never happened?

Of course, the shootings will always exist for the victims' loved ones, friends, spheres of influence. But for the rest of us – we can comfortably remove ourselves, dismiss the tragedies all because they happened to someone else and not us or the people we care about.

How is that ok though – just leaving the victims' loved ones to pick up the pieces of their lives, if that's even possible? A life in which they can have no expectation that this country will put a stop to mass shootings which stole their loved one?

Why must we resign ourselves to this? Because the politicians are gridlocked. It's hard for me to imagine a time since the Civil War that our country has been more bitterly divided than it is now. I am no great historian but I believe our country became as great as it is from America working together instead of against each other.

Though I have not always been consistent – I am a writer. I believe that in order to fulfill the destiny for which God put me on this earth, I need to write. This is what I can do in this cancer that tears America apart daily. Write. Use what I've got – which is my experience as a writer pretty much from the day I learned to write, and my experience as a 16-year lawyer.

But we don't need another book which does nothing more than argue politics and assign blame. We need SOLUTIONS! I don't expect this book to perform miracles. But I do expect it to create hope – I wouldn't waste my time with this otherwise. After my husband died, I spent a very long time in a writer's block. He was my rock who I leaned on for everything. Including my writing, of course. It took a lot to break out of that writer's block to get going on this book.

I'm writing this on the same day I learned of Kobe Bryant and his 13-year old daughter (same age as my son) perishing together in a helicopter crash. Yet another reminder, lest we needed more: Tomorrow is not promised. Let's love each other here and now while we can.

So I want to do what I can to not just free us from the control guns have over us, but to bring more love to the world. And what better way to do that than to confront something that steals and destroys so much love: guns.

Part One

The Unsanitized Reality of Murder

For over two hundred years after the enactment of the Second Amendment, the right to bear arms had a relatively simple meaning. This right was based on the long-standing "Castle Doctrine" – that people have a right to use simple firearms to defend their hearth and home. The policy behind the law was that people have access to guns suitable for civilian use, such as basic rifles and handguns, which would be sufficient for the defense of their homes and families.

But for the past two decades, the entire spirit and legal tradition of the Second Amendment has been thwarted and manipulated to meet the objectives of the NRA, the gun industry and criminals. These parties are now in favor of everyone, from the mentally ill to the criminal to the very young, having as many firearms as they want. The gun proponents also want no restrictions as to the types of weapons we can legally have. And as a result, civilians can now own assault weapons intended for military use[1] capable of firing as many as 950 rounds per minute.[2] The NRA also wants kids to arm up as early as possible and get hooked, before they can possibly get drawn away by childhood hobbies and pursuits such as arts-and-crafts, sports, fishing, playing with friends, and music.[3]

Laws like Stand Your Ground permit a person to legally gun someone down if he, like George Zimmerman, can convince the right people that he was in fear for his life or severe injury, even if this is a cold-blooded lie. SYG lets people legally shoot each other anywhere – they do not have to be in their home and they do not have a duty to retreat or diffuse the situation first.

The Trayvon Martin killing demonstrated that it has become far too easy for people to take each other's lives and do so legally, to boot. SYG is an encapsulation of the

---

[1] *See* http://www.handgunlaw.us/documents/DenverLaws.pdf.
[2] *See* http://ludingtoncitizen.ning.com/forum/topics/some-very-interesting-facts-about-assualt-weapons.
[3] *See* Tim Dickinson, *The Gun Industry's Deadly Addiction*, ROLLING STONE, Mar. 14, 2013, *available at* http://www.rollingstone.com/politics/news/the-gun-industrys-deadly-addiction-20130228.

influence that renegade justice has today. It is also a strong reflection of cowardice, not just in the context of confrontation and ways to diffuse them without deadly force, but also is a sad statement on what many Americans think of their fellow citizens and even people in their own communities and neighborhoods.

For example, George Zimmerman looked at Trayvon Martin not as a 17-year old boy walking home, but as an "asshole" who was "up to no good."[4] Zimmerman successfully used the SYG law as a predicate to, according to Florida prosecutors, pursue Martin, confront him and kill him under the guise of self-defense. People can be entitled to the SYG defenses even when they are the ones who started a fight in the first place if, like Zimmerman, they "reasonably believed" that they could be killed or seriously harmed. But why would you provoke a fight to begin with if

---

[4] Jeffrey Toobin, *The Facts In The Zimmerman Trial*, Daily Comment, THE NEW YORKER, July 16, 2013, *available at* http://www.newyorker.com/online/blogs/comment/2013/07/the-facts-in-the-george-zimmerman-trial.html.

you didn't want to be seriously injured or possibly killed? And if you decide to provoke a fight anyway, being aware of these risks as any reasonable person would be, don't you then assume the risks involved?

Second Amendment rights have exploded far beyond their original scope so that now the gun rights of a few translate to gun violence society as a whole must suffer. Many people are not aware of the true meaning and law behind the Second Amendment because the NRA constantly twists and distorts the truth. The truth is that Second Amendment rights are not absolute. People can in fact can be legally subjected to background and mental health checks before purchasing weapons. It is legal to place restrictions on the sale and use of assault weapons.

Even in the face of studies revealing that "84% of gun-owners and 74% of NRA members (vs. 90% of non-gun owners) supported requiring a universal background-check system for all gun sales,"[5] the Senate defeated a bipartisan legislative compromise to expand background checks for gun buyers, a ban on assault weapons, and a ban on high-capacity gun magazines on April 17, 2013.[6] The NRA triumphed over the defeat of the legislation, crowing they had succeeded in defending the rights of law-abiding citizens.[7] But what law-abiding citizen, no matter how many guns they have, wants to see more children murdered, being shot as many as eleven times each[8] eleven days before Christmas, as ornaments they had made were still drying on the classroom windowsill?[9]

---

[5] *See* Colleen L. Barry et al., *After Newtown—Public Opinion on Gun Policy and Mental Illness*, 368 NEW ENG. J. MED. 1077, 1077–108 (2013), *available at* http://www3.med.unipmn.it/papers/2013/NEJM/2013-03-21_nejm/nejmp1300512.pdf.

[6] Jonathan Weisman, *Senate Blocks Drive for Gun Control*, N. Y. TIMES, Apr. 17, 2013, *available at* http://www.nytimes.com/2013/04/18/us/politics/senate-obama-gun-control.html?pagewanted=all.

[7] National Rifle Association of America Institute for Legislative Action, *available at* http://www.nraila.org/about-nra-ila.aspx.

[8] James Barron, *Children Were All Shot Multiple Times with a Semiautomatic, Officials Say*, NEW YORK TIMES, Dec. 15, 2012, *available at* http://www.nytimes.com/2012/12/16/nyregion/gunman-kills-20-children-at-school-in-connecticut-28-dead-in-all.html?pagewanted=all.

[9] Ray Rivera, *Reliving Horror and Faint Hope at Massacre Site*, NEW YORK TIMES, Jan. 28, 2013, *available at* http://www.nytimes.com/2013/01/29/nyregion/horrors-of-newtown-shooting-scene-are-slow-to-fade.html?pagewanted=all&_r=0.

In the wake of the massacre at Sandy Hook Elementary, the NRA and their followers successfully deployed smokescreen and misinformation campaigns to confuse the public and divert their attention from taking effective action to combat gun violence. As a result, instead of people being galvanized by rage and grief over what had happened to these children and six of their teachers, cowardice took over. Too many people thought not about how such massacres are untenable and about doing everything in their power to help stop another one, but instead only thought about themselves ("What about my rights?" "These liberals are just making this stuff up so they can take my guns away." "To hell with everyone else, I only care about me").

The NRA effectively succeeded in steamrolling over the outpouring of emotion and grief over the massacre at Sandy Hook Elementary. Faced with the prospect of losing their precious guns, they even heckled Neil Heslin, whose son Jesse died in the Sandy Hook massacre, trying to silence the power of his words and grief at a Connecticut General Assembly task force hearing on January 29, 2013.[10] These cowards became deathly afraid of grief and emotion, because they knew these forces were probably their number one threat. Rarely has there been significant change to our laws and societal mores without the powerful catalyst of emotion.

The NRA continues to force-feed the public with the delusion that our Second Amendment rights are absolute. And given the number of people who actually believe that, too many Americans fight vehemently against any efforts of gun rights reform. They buy the NRA's claims that the government is coming to take all their guns away. And after the Sandy Hook massacre, they swarmed gun shops to grab all the assault weapons they could get their hands on. The

---

[10] The Associated Press, *Gun rights advocates heckle father of 6-year-old Newtown victim at Connecticut hearing*, NEW YORK DAILY NEWS, January 29, 2013, *available at* http://www.nydailynews.com/news/national/gun-rights-advocates-heckle-father-newtown-victim-article-1.1250124.

massacre (and mass shootings since) became, in sickening effect, *de facto* advertisements for assault weapons which caused a run on gun retailers because people just had to have that kind of power for themselves.

After the Newtown murders, some people advocated that the public should see the children's autopsy pictures for themselves, so that we could see the reality of gun violence and how we need to do everything within our power to stop the bloodshed. On one hand such an idea is sickening and appalling. But on the other hand, we need to face the facts and the reality. And every bullet that ravaged those children's bodies is the horrific, nightmarish reality. If we were forced to actually face the sickening excrement of our nightmarishly violent world, what would we do then? How would we act?

In the Bible's book of Exodus, God visited the following plagues upon the Egyptians: blood, frogs, lice or gnats, flies, pestilence, skin boils, hail, locusts, and darkness.[11]　None of these plagues were sufficient to convince the Pharaoh to free Moses and the Israelites. Only after the tenth and most severe plague, in which all Egyptian first-borns died[12] did the Pharaoh relent and permit the Israelites to leave. Though Pharaoh reversed himself a short time later,[13] it was only after he and other Egyptians suffered the pain of seeing their loved ones die that God's commands to let the Israelites go got through to the captors.

It did not have to come to that. If Pharaoh had come to his senses sooner, he and his fellow Egyptians would not have had to suffer the ultimate tragedy. What about us – what if we had come to our senses sooner? And what will be the consequences of us continuing to ignore these tragedies? Will losing a loved one be the only thing some people understand?

---

[11] Exodus 7-10, New International Version.
[12] Exodus 12:12, New International Version.
[13] Exodus 14:5-9, New International Version.

For many people, seeing is believing. What if everyone had to see the cold hard evidence of mass shootings: the pictures and videos of a mass shooting unfolding, the crime scenes, the bullet-ridden bodies, the autopsy photos? Many of us do not have to see images of gun violence victims to grasp the abominable horror and tragedy of what happened to them. But others, who dismiss the murders as mere incidents to the gun industry's cost of doing business clearly do not grasp the reality. For these people, the reality should not be sanitized any longer. They should be forced to come face to face with it.

To be sure, showing autopsy pictures or videos of murder victims, particularly children, would be too disturbing and traumatic for some people. And certainly, it could not be done unless the victims' family or authorized representatives gave permission. But the idea would not be to disgrace the victims, but to defend them. Sometimes there is nothing more powerful to defend a murder victim and their rights than to show them, show exactly what happened to them. Until then, some people will just not get it.

A perfect illustration of this is what happened after people around the world saw viral videos of police attacking and killing George Floyd, a black man, on March 25, 2020. These videos revealed Minneapolis police officer Derek Chauvin, a white man, kneeling on Mr. Floyd's neck for at least eight minutes and 15 seconds.[14] As he lay dying, Mr. Floyd repeatedly called out for his mother.[15] He pleaded at least 16 times that he could not breathe. A bystander attempted to remonstrate with the police perpetrators when one of them claimed Mr. Floyd was fine: "[He] ain't fine...Get him off the ground...You could have put him in

14 Evan Hill, Ainara Tiefenthäler, Christiaan Triebert, Drew Jordan, Haley Willis and Robin Stein, *How George Floyd Was Killed in Police Custody*, NEW YORK TIMES, May 31, 2020, *available at* https://www.nytimes.com/2020/05/31/us/george-floyd-investigation.html.
15 Killing of George Floyd. (n.d.). In Wikipedia. Retrieved July 4, 2020, from https://en.m.wikipedia.org/wiki/Killing_of_George_Floyd

the car by now. He's not resisting arrest or nothing. You're enjoying it. Look at you. Your body language explains it."

The videos of George Floyd's killing at the hands of police went viral, triggering a new civil rights revolution which may be the largest movement in United States history.[16] And why? It transcended racial barriers and other divisions. This was a human issue that reasonable people could agree upon. It was unconscionable that police officers could do this, when they had already gotten away with it for far too long. We felt the pain of George Floyd's death. Mothers heard him calling out for his mama and embraced him in their hearts just as if he were their own. Black people, along with people of all races, rose up and in the short space of days and weeks, transformed our society and changed the course of history.

---

[16] Larry Buchanan, Quoctrung Bui and Jugal K. Patel, *Black Lives Matter May Be the Largest Movement in U.S. History*, NEW YORK TIMES, July 3, 2020, *available at* https://www.nytimes.com/interactive/2020/07/03/us/george-floyd-protests-crowd-size.html.

If only it did not take experiencing the pain of death ourselves to understand the pain that families of murder victims feel. But for some people unfortunately, this is the only thing they will understand. Make no mistake – nothing in this book should be read to suggest that anyone, no matter what their views, should ever have to suffer losing a loved one to murder. But for some people, only after they actually see murder victims for themselves will they have any concept of the reality of gun violence.

Sometimes, seeing the unadulterated truth of murder with our own eyes can be paying the highest honor to the murder victims. Sometimes, only after seeing this truth will people be galvanized to action, sometimes action that changes the entire balance of power and course of history.

Marc Antony understood this well as he presided over Julius Caesar's funeral, after Caesar had been murdered by conspirators, led by Brutus and Cassius. Brutus had been a close personal friend of Caesar's, which prompted Caesar's famous last words as Brutus' knife joined all the others: "*Et tu, Brute*? Then fall Caesar!"[17]

When the Romans first assembled for Caesar's funeral, they were convinced of the conspirators' version of events, that Caesar was a tyrant and that they were better off without him. As Brutus told the throng,

> Had you rather Caesar were living and
> die all slaves, than that Caesar were dead, to live
> all free men? As Caesar loved me, I weep for him;
> as he was fortunate, I rejoice at it; as he was
> valiant, I honour him: but, as he was ambitious, I
> slew him. There is tears for his love; joy for his
> fortune; honour for his valour; and death for his
> ambition. Who is here so base that would be a
> bondman? If any, speak; for him have I offended.
> Who is here so rude that would not be a Roman? If

---

[17] Shakespeare, William, *The Tragedy of Julius Caesar* (3.1.1286).

any, speak; for him have I
offended. Who is here so
vile that will not love his
country? If any, speak;
for him have I offended. I

pause for a reply.[18]

The crowd then eagerly assured Brutus that there was no

one whom he had offended. When Mark Antony took the

pulpit to preside over Caesar's funeral (which Brutus had

been sure to inform the crowd that this was only by the

conspirators' leave[19]) everyone below was fully convinced of

what a tyrant Caesar had been. Antony was fully aware of

this and with his opening statements of "Friends, Romans,

countrymen, lend me your ears; I come to bury Caesar, not

to praise him," he deftly got the crowd to agree with him

from the outset.[20] And as every good salesperson knows,

you are always working toward the next "yes."

So now that Antony had gotten the crowd's first

"yes," he continued to smoothly dovetail his defense of

---

[18] *Id.* at 3.2.1556-1568.
[19] *Id.* at 1595-98.
[20] *See id.* at 1617-18.

Caesar into Brutus' earlier proclamations that it was

Caesar's ambition which had cost him his life:

> He was my friend, faithful and just to me:
> But Brutus says he was ambitious;
> And Brutus is an honourable man.
> He hath brought many captives home to
> Rome
> Whose ransoms did the general coffers fill:
> Did this in Caesar seem ambitious?
> When that the poor have cried, Caesar hath
> wept:
> Ambition should be made of sterner stuff:
> Yet Brutus says he was ambitious;
> And Brutus is an honourable man.
> You all did see that on the Lupercal
> I thrice presented him a kingly crown,
> Which he did thrice refuse: was this
> ambition?
> Yet Brutus says he was ambitious;
> And, sure, he is an honourable man.
> I speak not to disprove what Brutus spoke,
> But here I am to speak what I do know.
> You all did love him once, not without cause:
> What cause withholds you then, to mourn
> for him?
> O judgment! thou art fled to brutish beasts,
> And men have lost their reason. Bear with
> me;
> My heart is in the coffin there with Caesar,
> And I must pause till it come back to me.[21]

---

[21] *Id.* at 1629-51.

With this the crowd began to realize the error in their thinking about Caesar, some even going so far as to say that if indeed Caesar was not ambitious "some will dear abide it"[22] (or pay for it, in modern parlance). When Antony resumed his remarks, he was well aware of how the tide was turning in his favor, and stepped up his suggestive selling, saying

> O masters, if I were disposed
> to stir
> Your hearts and minds to
> mutiny and rage,
> I should do Brutus wrong,
> and Cassius wrong,
> Who, you all know, are
> honourable men:
> I will not do them wrong; I
> rather choose
> To wrong the dead, to wrong
> myself and you,
> Than I will wrong such
>
> honourable men.[23]

But before going too far, Antony employed the well-known sales "takeaway" and instead turned the crowd's attention to Caesar's will. As a backdrop for Antony's presentation of

---

[22] *Id.* at 1659.
[23] *Id.* at 1666-72.

the will, he invited the crowd to draw nearer to Caesar's body, upon which Antony said "Let me show you him that made the will."[24]

Antony then displayed each of Caesar's knife wounds to the crowd, naming the conspirators who had dealt them:

> Look, in this place ran
> Cassius' dagger through:
> See what a rent the envious
> Casca made:
> Through this the well-beloved
> Brutus stabb'd;
> And as he pluck'd his cursed
> steel away,
> Mark how the blood of Caesar
> follow'd it,
> As rushing out of doors, to be
> resolved
> If Brutus so unkindly knock'd,
> or no;
> For Brutus, as you know, was
> Caesar's angel:
> Judge, O you gods, how
> dearly Caesar loved him!
> This was the most unkindest
> cut of all;
> For when the noble Caesar
> saw him stab,

---

[24] *Id.* at 1703.

Ingratitude, more strong than
traitors' arms,
Quite vanquish'd him: then
burst his mighty heart;
And, in his mantle muffling
up his face,
Even at the base of Pompey's
statua,
Which all the while ran
blood, great Caesar fell.
O, what a fall was there, my
countrymen!
Then I, and you, and all of us
fell down,
Whilst bloody treason
flourish'd over us.
O, now you weep; and, I
perceive, you feel
The dint of pity: these are
gracious drops.
Kind souls, what, weep you
when you but behold
Our Caesar's vesture
wounded? Look you here,
Here is himself, marr'd, as

you see, with traitors.[25]

These last three lines describe how Antony removed

Caesar's robes so that the throng could look upon his naked,

lifeless body and the unadulterated extent of his mortal

wounds. Presented with this sight, the crowd was

[25] *Id.* at 1719-42.

transformed: "O piteous spectacle!" "O noble Caesar!" "O woful day!" "O traitors, villains!" "O most bloody sight!" they cried out in anguish and mourning.[26] Then, their sadness quickly turned to anger and that anger quickly turned to action: "We will be revenged," "Revenge! About! Seek! Burn! Fire! Kill! Slay! Let not a traitor live!"[27]

Even now, Antony maintained his diplomacy, seemingly distancing himself from the crowd's sudden resolution to exact revenge on the conspirators. He reminded them

> Why, friends, you go to do
> you know not what:
> Wherein hath Caesar thus
> deserved your loves?
> Alas, you know not: I must
> tell you then:
> You have forgot the will I told
>
> you of.[28]

---

[26] *Id.* at 1743-7.
[27] *Id.* at 1748-50.
[28] *Id.* at 1780-3.

Antony revealed all that Caesar had bequeathed to the Roman citizenry, such as "seventy-five drachmas" to each citizen, "all his walks, His private arbours and new-planted orchards, On this side Tiber; he hath left them you, And to your heirs for ever, common pleasures, To walk abroad, and recreate yourselves."[29] With Antony's final appeal to the crowd "Here was a Caesar! when comes such another?"[30] the crowd's fury was ignited anew, and from then on there was no stopping them.

This is not to say that we should harm others or answer gun violence in kind. But the point is that we need to pay attention to the spin people put on murder and tragedies to suit their own purposes. Brutus, like the NRA, succeeded in deluding the public by claiming that he had to murder Caesar to save the Romans from his tyranny. This distracted them from the reality of the murder and from mourning Caesar. Conversely, Antony restored the

---

[29] *Id.* at 1785-96.
[30] *Id.* at 1797.

humanity of the victim which had been stolen by the conspirators. He began by creating the illusion that he agreed with the conspirators, getting the people's goodwill through the backdoor. Then Antony gradually infused emotion back into the people, reminding them of all Caesar had done for his subjects. Finally, he drove his messages home with a powerful demonstrative aid – revealing Caesar's naked, lifeless body rent with fatal knife wounds. It was only then that the crowd's grief erupted to the point that it turned to anger, then action.

The NRA and their followers play hardball of the worst kind. To fight back, supporters of solutions against gun violence need to play hardball of their own, on their own terms. We need to see the actual, literal, bloody, gruesome consequences of mass shootings with our own eyes. Some may call it exploiting and politicizing the dead. But in reality, it is probably one of the strongest weapons we have in our arsenal. We must answer the blood of the victims that cries out from the ground – the children and teachers of Sandy Hook Elementary and Marjorie Stoneman Douglass, the Las Vegas concertgoers, the Colorado Batman moviegoers, so many more...how many more?

Part Two

The Truth About Second Amendment Rights

The NRA loves to deploy disinformation strategies and stoke fear. They do so by perpetuating such myths as "The government is coming to take away all of your guns!" "Our Second Amendment rights are absolute!" and "Guns aren't the problem – this is the fault of the mental health system."

Proving the falsity of these myths is actually fairly simple. It only requires reading the Supreme Court's latest word on Second Amendment rights, in the 2008 case of *District of Columbia v. Heller*, which among other things provides that yes, we as citizens do have a right to bear arms and no, Second Amendment rights are not absolute.

This summary of the case provides many of its key highlights. In *District of Columbia v. Heller*, the Supreme Court considered whether a "District of Columbia prohibition on the possession of usable handguns in the home violates the Second Amendment to the Constitution.[31]

---

[31] *Dist. of Columbia v. Heller*, 554 U.S. 570 (2008).

The respondent in the case, Dick Heller, was a D.C. special police officer authorized to carry a handgun while on duty at the Thurgood Marshall Judiciary Building.[32] The District of Columbia (the "District") denied Mr. Heller's application for a registration certificate to keep a handgun at home.[33] Mr. Heller then filed suit in federal court seeking to enjoying the District from enforcing its prohibitions against handguns in the home on Second Amendment grounds.[34] The trial court dismissed Mr. Heller's complaint. However, the appellate court reversed, finding that the Second Amendment conveys the right to individuals to bear arms, and further invalidated the District's requirement that any firearms in the home be disabled.[35] The Supreme Court granted certiorari.[36]

As stated by the Second Amendment: "A well regulated Militia, being necessary to the security of a free

---

[32] *Id.* at 575.
[33] *Id.*
[34] *Id.* at 575-576.
[35] *Id.* at 576.
[36] *Id.*

State, the right of the people to keep and bear Arms, shall not be infringed."[37] The court noted that constitutional words and phrases were intended to be used in their normal and ordinary meaning, as opposed to technical meaning, so as to be better understood by voters.[38]

The Court rejected the position taken by the petitioners and the dissent which argued that the Second Amendment protects only the right to possess and carry a firearm in connection with military service.[39] The Court then launched into an extensive study in linguistics, largely open to interpretation, as to how it chose to construe each word in the Second Amendment. For example, in defining the word "arms," the Court looked to the 1773 edition of Samuel Johnson's dictionary which defined "arms" as "weapons of offence" or "armour of defence."[40] The Court found that definition to also apply as of its decision date.[41]

---

[37] Id.
[38] Id.
[39] Id. at 577.
[40] Id. at 581, citing to 1 Dictionary of the English Language 106 (4th ed.) (reprinted 1978).
[41] 554 U.S. at 581.

The majority eschewed the petitioners and the dissent's hybrid definition of the phrase "bear arms" where it was only permissible to do so in the service of an organized militia.[42] In so holding, the Court noted that "[n]o dictionary has ever adopted that definition, and we have been apprised of no source that indicates that it carried that meeting at the time of the founding."[43] Together with this finding and the linguistic analysis, the Court concluded that the Second Amendment conveys the individual right to possess and carry weapons in case of confrontation.[44] The Court made brief references to several of its prior cases dealing with the Second Amendment, such as *United States v. Cruikshank, Presser v. Illinois* and *United States v. Miller,* and found that none of them precluded such a reading of the Second Amendment. On the contrary, the Court often read these cases is ultimately supporting its *Heller* rulings.[45]

---

[42] *Id.* at 586.
[43] *Id.*
[44] *Id.* at 592.
[45] *See id.* at 619-625.

More to the point, the Court held: "There seems to us no doubt, on the basis of both text and history, that the Second Amendment conferred an individual right to keep and bear arms. Of course, the right was not unlimited, just as the First Amendment's right of free speech was not. Thus, we do not read the Second Amendment to protect the right of citizens to carry arms for any sort of confrontation, just as we do not read the First Amendment to protect the right of citizens to speak for any purpose."[46]

The Court stated that it would turn the limitations upon the individual right after it determined whether the Preparatory Clause of the 2nd Amendment comported with its interpretation of the operative Clause.[47] However the Court never did spell out any specific limitations to the right, other than to suggest to some general guidelines but nothing that can explicitly put a citizen on notice of exactly

---

[46] *Id.* at 595 (citation omitted).
[47] *Id.*

what types of weapons go beyond the scope of the Second Amendment.

However the Court does, in several instances, state that Second Amendment rights are for defensive purposes only.[48] In reviewing several pre-Second Amendment state constitutional Provisions, the Court's reading was that they secured an individual right to bear arms for the defensive purposes.[49] Likewise, during discussions of passing the Fourteenth Amendment, "Senator Pomeroy described as one of the three 'indispensable' 'safeguards of liberty...under the Constitution' a man's 'right to bear arms for the defense of himself and family and his homestead.'"[50] Furthermore, "[n]o doubt, a citizen who keeps a gun or pistol under judicious precautions, practices in safe places the use of it, and in due time teaches his sons to do the same, exercises his individual right. No doubt, a person whose residence or

---

[48] *See, e.g., id.* at 602.
[49] *Id.*
[50] *Id.* at 616, *citing to* Cong. Globe, 39th Cong., 1st Sess., 1182 (1866).

duties involve peculiar peril may keep a pistol for prudent self-defence."[51]

In opposing the majority's decision, Justice Stevens relied heavily on the Court's decision in *United States v. Miller.*[52] While rejecting most of Justice Stevens' argument (for the proposition that one reason for the defendant's indictment there was that they were bearing weapons for non-military use), the majority did state: "Rather, it was that the type of weapon at issue was not eligible for Second Amendment protection: '[i]n the absence of any evidence tending to show that possession or use of a 'shotgun having a barrel of less than eighteen inches in length' at this time has some reasonable relationship to the preservation or efficiency of a well regulated militia, we cannot say that the Second Amendment guarantees the right to keep and bear such an instrument."[53]

---

[51] 554 U.S. at 619, *citing to* B. Abbott, Judge and Jury: A Popular Explanation of the Leading Topics in the Law of the Land 333 (1880).
[52] 307 U.S. 174 (1939).
[53] *Id.* at 622, *citing to Miller*, 307 U. S. at 178 (alteration in original).

The *Heller* court declined to provide specific guidance as to what sorts of weapons are not protected by the Second Amendment. The Court did construe *Miller* to say that "the Second Amendment does not protect those weapons not typically possessed by law-abiding citizens for lawful purposes, such as short-barreled shotguns. That accords with the historical understanding of the scope of the right."[54]

The Court went on to say that the Second Amendment is not the only constitutional provision which has taken a long time to elucidate upon as to the scope of rights provided therein.[55] For example, the Court did not find that a law violated the First Amendment's guarantee of free speech until 1931, almost 150 years after its ratification.[56]

Contrary to many modern views such as those of the NRA and its fan base, "[l]ike most rights, the right secured by the Second Amendment is not unlimited. From

---

[54] 554 U.S. at 625 (citation omitted).
[55] *Id.* at 625
[56] *Id.* at 625-626.

Blackstone through the 19th-century cases, commentators and courts routinely explained that the right was not a right to keep and carry any weapon whatsoever in any manner whatsoever and for whatever purpose."[57] Although the Court did little to expound on limitations of Second Amendment rights, it did specify that "nothing in our opinion should be taken to cast doubt on longstanding prohibitions on the possession of firearms by felons and the mentally ill, or laws forbidding the carrying of firearms in sensitive places such as schools and government buildings, or laws imposing conditions and qualifications on the commercial sale of arms."[58]

The Court also stated that dangerous and unusual weapons should be excluded from Second Amendment protections as the Second Amendment arose in part from able-bodied citizens being able to join the military and using such lawful weapons as they already possessed at

---

[57] *Id.* at 626.
[58] *Id.* at 626-627 (citation omitted).

home.[59] The Court stopped short of saying assault weapons should be banned because the same type of weapons that were in common in the 18th century would be less effective today against modern-day bombers and tanks.[60] In response to the petitioners' argument that handguns could be banned as long as other firearms were allowed, the Court stated that "[i]t is enough to note, as we have observed, that the American people have considered the handgun to be the quintessential self-defense weapon.[61]

In closing, the Court addressed Justice Breyer's contentions that the majority had left "so many applications of the right to keep and bear arms in doubt, and for not providing extensive historical justification for those regulations of the right that we deem permissible."[62] The Court offered the justification that the *Heller* decision represented the Court's first in-depth examination of the Second Amendment (despite the previous Supreme Court

---

[59] *Id.* at 627.
[60] *Id.*
[61] *Id.* at 629.
[62] *Id.* at 635.

cases examined earlier to ensure they did not conflict) and that the public should not expect the instant decision to clarify the entire field of Second Amendment law, and that there would be plenty of time for the court to address ambiguities of the right later.[63] Consequently, the Court upheld the Appellate Court's decision in ruling that the District's ban on handgun possession violated the Second Amendment, as did its prohibition against rendering any lawful firearm in the home operable for the purpose of immediate self-defense.[64]

While the Court claimed it took gun violence problems in this country seriously, it stated that banning handgun ownership was not an option due to constitutional guarantees.[65] The Court further disclaimed responsibility for considering the possibility that the Second Amendment is now extinct "in a society where our standing army is the pride of our Nation, where well-trained police forces

---

[63] *Id.*
[64] *Id.*
[65] *Id.* at 636.

provide personal security, and where gun violence is a serious problem."[66] The court admitted these issues were debatable but demurred that to strike down the Second Amendment is not within the Court's role to do.[67]

This last sentence alone should take away a central premise of NRA propaganda – stoking fear that the government is coming to take away your guns. Not only did the Supreme Court disclaim any responsibility for whether the Second Amendment exists or not, it also bolstered the fact that we have a Constitutional right to bear arms (irrespective of military service) and established that handguns are commonly accepted as self-defense weapons. This seems to leave room for later opinions or laws as to the legality of assault weapons, as they go well beyond the scope of self-defense and what has historically been sufficient in that regard. But there is nothing in this opinion, which is the current "last word" on Second Amendment rights,

---

[66] *Id.*
[67] *Id.*

which supports the idea that the government is coming to

take away your guns, even if you do own assault weapons.

Conclusion

We have seen this vicious cycle play out over and over again:

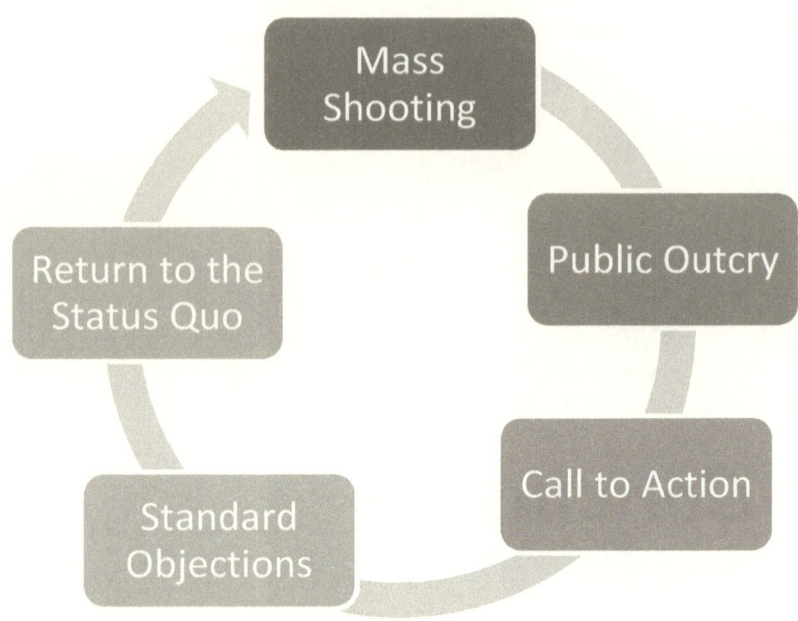

1) Mass shooting;

2) Public outcry;

3) People being galvanized to take action and make sure something like this never happens again while simultaneously being accused of others of trying to use a tragedy for political gain;

4) The public resolve to do something about this tragedy (other than the requisite thoughts and prayers) is overcome by the standard objections;

5) We return to the status quo;

6) Another mass shooting occurs, setting the cycle off all over again...

As the Prevention Institute States, "[p]art of our healing must be the conviction that we will do everything in our power to keep these tragedies from happening in a nation that continues to face a pandemic of gun violence."[68] We must work to prevent not only the mass shooting that are splattered all over the news but also the lesser-known gun killings that claimed more than 30,000 lives every year.[69]

The Prevention Institute points out that every time a mass shooting occurs, we tend to have a tunnel vision approach in that any prevention efforts are directed to the venue type where the shooting took place. For example,

---

[68] https://www.preventioninstitute.org/focus-areas/preventing-violence-and-reducing-injury/preventing-violence-advocacy
[69] *Id.*

after the mass murders in Parkland, Florida, the dialogue centered on how to prevent gun violence in schools only. However, the Prevention Institute urges that we must insist on that same level of safety for our places of worship, shopping malls, movie theaters, concert venues, nightclubs, workplaces, neighborhoods, and homes.

Really, what venue is not immune to being penetrated by gun violence? What amount of security is enough? And at what point is it cost prohibitive for individuals and organizations? We cannot all afford the security systems in details enjoyed by the wealthy and celebrities. And even then, no security system is foolproof. Many of the mass shooting sites did have at least some level of security.

To break free of the vicious cycle of gun violence, we must reject as false the disinformation strategies deployed by the NRA and their supporters. As stated earlier, the NRA likes to stoke fear by claiming that the government is coming for our guns. This is a popular fear-mongering statement that only catalyzes people to go out and buy more guns, more assault guns, more weapons of war that have no place in the realm of reasonable self-defense.

In terms of gun violence prevention, we are working from quite a deficit. The damage has already been done in terms of how many weapons are in the hands of Americans, including those with the capacity to murder or commit mass shootings. So a big question is, Where Do We Go From Here?

And anytime it is remotely suggested that people should not have certain weapons, this causes another outcry and proponents of those weapons dig their heels in deeper. Guns become even more attractive of a commodity. Sadly, mass shootings themselves become a de facto advertisement for guns, assault weapons in particular. People run out and buy more for multiple reasons. They're scared for their own safety. They think the government is going to take away these guns so they run out and buy more while they still can.

So what do we do now? A lot of it comes down to our society. And how that society shapes these killers. They were once screaming babies like you and me. Contrary to the popular saying, there is no such thing as "Natural Born Killers." So how did they become that way? And how we can how can we prevent them from becoming that way?

This is hard because now we are trying to control the free will of individuals. Individuals will often do what is in their capacity to do. And especially since it is so easy to obtain guns, including weapons of war, if a mass shooter has the free will to commit mass murder, very little is standing in his way.[70]

So, recognizing the limitations in trying to control the free will of individuals, especially when this country makes it so easy for them to become mass shooters if they so desire, we must use defensive strategies. We must protect ourselves. Because like it or not, the Wild West is

[70] "His" because the vast majority of mass shooters are men.

back in many ways. That is what we have regressed to. Anyone, anywhere, may be carrying a gun and can use them at will.

Therefore, it is logical for law-abiding citizens to exercise their Second Amendment right for self-defense. Concealed carry permits also make sense. However, not one mass shooting yet has been prevented by a good guy with a gun.

This takes us back to the beginning of the book, and our attitude about mass killings. We have become more callous, hostile and selfish in the last two decades, and the gun violence reflects that. These same attitudes also let white police officers kill black people at will, unchecked and without accountability, for far too long. What did it take to finally break our indifference? Maybe it was more than just the videos of George Floyd and the killer's knee in his neck, because far too many other black people were killed by police who got away with it, even when these killings were caught on camera as well. Maybe it was a combination of the COVID-19, sitting at home going out of our minds, and some other straw that broke the camel's back. But whatever it was, the indifference, selfishness, callousness was broken. People rose up and did the right thing. They stood up for justice. We can do it again. And as many times as it takes to put more love back into this world, until these mass shootings become a relic of a barbaric age.

www.ingramcontent.com/pod-product-compliance
Lightning Source LLC
Chambersburg PA
CBHW030530220526
45463CB00007B/2778